To April
may this
be a blessing
to you.
m. Gregory.

MW01289579

I Think I Gave GOD A Ride To Work Last Night

A Book of Emotionally Charged True Stories of Love, Family, and Miracles

Morton Gregory

BALBOA.
PRESS
A DIVISION OF HAY HOUSE

Balboa Press books may be ordered through booksellers or by contacting:

Balboa Press
A Division of Hay House
1663 Liberty Drive
Bloomington, IN 47403
www.balboapress.com
1 (877) 407-4847

Because of the dynamic nature of the Internet, any web addresses or links contained in this book may have changed since publication and may no longer be valid. The views expressed in this work are solely those of the author and do not necessarily reflect the views of the publisher, and the publisher hereby disclaims any responsibility for them.

The author of this book does not dispense medical advice or prescribe the use of any technique as a form of treatment for physical, emotional, or medical problems without the advice of a physician, either directly or indirectly. The intent of the author is only to offer information of a general nature to help you in your quest for emotional and spiritual well-being. In the event you use any of the information in this book for yourself, which is your constitutional right, the author and the publisher assume no responsibility for your actions.

Any people depicted in stock imagery provided by Thinkstock are models, and such images are being used for illustrative purposes only.
Certain stock imagery © Thinkstock.

Print information available on the last page.

ISBN: 978-1-5043-3611-6 (sc)
ISBN: 978-1-5043-3613-0 (hc)
ISBN: 978-1-5043-3612-3 (e)

Library of Congress Control Number: 2015910979

Balboa Press rev. date: 09/30/2015

Dedication Page

I would like to dedicate this book to my wife Brenda, who has been my partner in everything we do and has always filled my life with love. I realized a long time ago how lucky I am to have her.

I would also like to dedicate this book to my children and grandchildren, who will never realize what a love I have for them.

And a thank you to my maker for giving me such a strong compassion for other people which is truly a gift to me. I am blessed.

My heart felt thank you goes out to my dear friend Brittany Bush for helping me along the way during the publishing process. I could not have done it without her!!

I Think I
Gave God a
Ride to Work
Last Night

The story began when I decided I was going to write a prayer to God every morning. I think God comes to us in many forms. A lot of times, we don't recognize him. I think he just checks in to see how we are doing and how we are treating others, especially ones in need. I think my wife and I passed the test last night, and I hope God smiled.

Since I started writing my prayer each morning, I have felt such a connection to him. My days go better, and I look at others in a different way. I think I am beginning to see them as God does. However, God has some pretty funky outfits; you would never guess it was him. Sometimes, he hangs around in some weird places, like in that men's room at the Opryland Hotel in Nashville, Tennessee, where he was disguised as a janitor.

I was standing at a urinal, doing what men do at a urinal, when out of the blue, God said, "Give him a tip." I said to myself, "Really?" So me being me I reached into my pocket and gave the janitor a ten-dollar tip. You would think I gave him a hundred dollars.

The man thanked me over and over again. I said, "You are welcome. You are doing a good job."

He said, "Bless you, sir. Bless you."

I was there on a business trip. I was wearing an expensive suit, and he acted like I was someone with money and prestige. In fact, I should have been a servant to him. When I was leaving, he said thank you again. He explained that he did try to do a good job. At that point, I told him it showed.

I know I saw God that day. As I walked out of the bathroom, a feeling came over me. I knew it was God, and I began to cry tears of joy. I couldn't control myself. When I realized what had happened, I ran back to the men's room, but no one was there.

That was many years ago, but I will never forget that moment.

To get back to last night and my morning letter to God, I asked God to allow me to be a blessing to someone that day. He usually does, and last night was no different. It was raining cats and dogs. My wife and I were on our way to dinner. We saw a skinny little girl with long hair, flip-flops, a McDonald's uniform, and an umbrella. She looked like she had a long way to go. My wife and I turned around, went back, and asked if we could give her a ride. She jumped into our car and said, "Thank you. No one has ever done anything like this for me. You are such a blessing to me." She kept repeating that during the drive.

I hadn't seen her working at McDonald's before and I haven't seen her again since that night. I am smart enough to know from that day in the men's room that we were the blessed ones that night in the rain. Thank you, God.

What Would Grandpa Spear Do?

Grandpa Spear was a quiet man. Even though he never saved any damsels in distress, set any records, or caught any bad guys, he was a hero. His eyes always had a gleam that warmed your soul and made everything all right.

When I was young, I would go to his camp as much as possible. It was a special place on a quiet pond back in the woods. We'd fish, and when the bullheads were biting, you could catch one after another. The bullhead were very small, but the meat was so sweet and tender. I think the bullheads in Sterling Pond are like life: sweet and tender if you taste. Yet, they also have horns that can stick you. You must respect that and handle them carefully.

From the way he handled life and bullhead, I could tell Grandpa Spear always knew this. After we would get a bucket of fish, we would put our poles away and go into camp for the "cleaning of the fish" ceremony. I call it this because it was always the same. Grandpa would stand bent over the sink in the tiny little kitchen and clean the fish while Grandma and I sat at the kitchen table and teased him about what a good job he was doing. This would always get the same reaction. Grandpa would threaten to make us do it. Knowing Grandpa, we were not too worried. We knew he loved doing it for us as much as we loved teasing him about it. When the fish were cleaned, Grandma would roll them in cracker crumbs and fry them in butter. I would eat them as fast as she could get them out of the frying pan. Grandpa would always say he didn't want any, but we knew he really wanted to save them for us.

As I grew older and discovered teenage girls, fast cars, and drive-in movies, the times at camp became less frequent, but the memories are something I will always have. Sometimes I close my eyes and swear I can still smell the bullhead cooking, see Grandpa smiling, and smell the cleanliness of Grandpa's flannel shirts that I used to wrap up in to protect myself from the night air at the campfire.

When life gets a little hard, I sometimes wish I could go back to the safety of those times. I think Grandpa knew those days would come when I was older because he gave me more than childhood memories on Sterling Pond. He taught me more than how to catch bullhead, which side of the tree the moss grows on, and what critters made sounds at night. He taught me integrity by having it. He taught me about helping others by always unselfishly doing it. He also taught me the importance of sticking to our values by never wavering from his own. Grandpa never made any big speeches—just small statements of action.

I thank God for Grandpa Spear and my times growing up on Sterling Pond. I know I am very lucky to have had those times, and I hope someone in your life has given you the gift of the same times and lessons. If not, I am sure Grandpa wouldn't mind if you do what I do when you are faced with one of life's important decisions.

When all else fails, pause for a minute and ask, yourself the question. "What would Grandpa Spear do?"

Freckles, Pigtails, and Dreams

The innocence of our youth! When dreams are free and anything is possible. All the I-want-tos: I want to be a policeman. I want to be a fireman. I want to be an astronaut. I want to be a nurse, doctor, or writer. Better yet, I want to be a movie star. We can dress up and play any role or travel anyplace we want in our minds. No one told us not to be silly.

The problem started when they thought it was time for us to learn about the real world. It all started in kindergarten. All of a sudden, our coloring had to stay within the lines. Well, I decided I was going to be different. They said, "You can do this. You can't do that." And it didn't really fit my way of thinking. I was a free spirit with a mind and dreams of my own. If I wanted to grow up to be a fireman, what did that have to do with the alphabet? And what if I wanted to be a movie star? I had all the schooling I needed. I could practice all day at home. In the morning, I could be a cowboy, and in the afternoon, I could be a policeman.

Well, I made it through kindergarten all right, but when first grade came, I had had enough of the real-world stuff. This was someone else's real world, not mine. My dad would drop me off in front of the school, and the rodeo would begin. I was the wild mustang that needed to be roped and tied. Dad would drop me off at the front, and I would run out the back door as fast as my little legs would carry me! The teachers, I still believe to this day, thought I would give up easily, but no way! School was not my idea of how I was going to spend my days. So the chase was on. The four first grade teachers, a janitor, and Billy Dawson—one of those brownnosers in the second grade—would catch me and send me the principal's office. I didn't mind too much because by the time they told me I couldn't do this every day, school was in session. I had already missed the first hour.

It really began to get interesting when they started sending me down to Mr. Billings. He was the guy who makes you put the different-shaped blocks into the different holes and then timed you doing it. I think Mr. Billings was the school psychologist. That was okay because I would just pretend I was a super spy and Mr. Billings was the mafia. I really knew what he was up to, but I wasn't about to let him know that I knew.

Finally, after Mr. Billings, they just let me sit in my brother's fifth-grade classroom all year and decided to allow me to repeat first grade the next year.

So there I was in first grade all over again. This time, it was different. I was beginning to see that there were too many of them against only me. I started to do all the things you are supposed to do, and life, as it was, went on. The dreams became less believable, and the rules became stricter. All the way through school, we had to have reading, writing, and math. When high school came along, we needed to add language and earth science.

Like the majority, you just followed along with the real world. People told you that you can't do this, you have to do that, or this is the only right answer—and you don't argue about it. After we go through high school, we head off to college or work, all trained for the real world. The observation that has come to me is that we have messed up. Yes, I know we have to have rules in society, but I also think we have to look back at the "I want tos." The way I see it in the so-called real world, there are too many of us going to see too many people like Mr. Billings.

Maybe we need to introduce "Self-Esteem 101" as a mandatory class, or "Goal Setting 101." Language and history are okay if we have the time, but we can't afford to give up self-esteem and goal setting. We need to take the freckled and pigtailed youth of today and let them dream. If they color out of the lines, compliment them on their choice or colors. Where would we be if Thomas Edison hadn't had the self-esteem to believe in the electric lightbulb or if Henry Ford hadn't built the Model T?

These guys colored outside the real world's lines. The people who tell you your dreams are silly are living in the real world of Mr. Billings. The people who hold on to their dreams are living in the world of Mr. Edison and Mr. Ford. Which one are we going to teach our youth to live in by example?

By the way, what you are reading is one of those famous "I want tos" that everyone said was silly. I decided to live in the real world of Mr. Ford and Mr. Edison. I kept on writing. Billy Dawson, the brownnoser, probably has appointments with Mr. Billings on Monday, Wednesday, and Friday at ten o'clock.

The Little
Red Ashtray

The story began when I was four years old. I think we all have memories of the good times and the challenges in our lives. We never forget the sweet and innocent moments. I am sixty years old now, and just this morning, I picked up the little red ashtray and held it in my hand as softly as I hold it in my heart. It was a Mother's Day present I bought with my own money for my mom. I knew she would love it, but I never realized how much until years later.

I always wondered why she displayed it in the formal dining room with all the expensive, limited pieces of art. Now I know why. I know the ashtray, to her, was the most valuable piece in the whole display—but not because of its beauty. That ashtray was more than a piece of glass; it was a piece of my heart. Her little boy loved her. The funny thing was that my mother hated smoking. As a little boy, they never told me it was an ashtray. I just thought it was the most beautiful red candy dish I had ever seen, and in a way, it was.

As a teenager, I started smoking. Like all my friends, I was probably trying to be cool. My mom didn't like it, but like most people who get hooked, it is one of the hardest things to stop doing.

When my mom died and all the things were being given away to her children, the only thing I asked for was that little red ashtray that my mom never put aside to make room for the expensive things. I had a very hard time accepting my mom's death.

I decided to give my mom one more Mother's Day gift. I am sure she loved it as much as she loved that beautiful red ashtray. I quit smoking in honor of her that Mother's Day, and I have not smoked another cigarette in twenty-two years.

Dead Man's Run

I would die for her. I think any normal American teenage boy from anywhere in the USA—with hormones racing faster than the land speed record set in Utah Flats—has heard or made this statement. At age eleven, I thought it was the yuckiest thing I had ever heard, and I swore I would never make such a geek statement. At age sixteen, Mary Forbes turned me into a liar. I not only made the statement, and I almost literally acted it out.

The story all began on the ski slopes. Mary belonged to one of *those* families. When the kids were babies, instead of teaching them how to walk, they skipped right to putting on skis. She had been skiing longer than I had been walking, and I was six months older. Every weekend, my friends and I would load up my car with skis, poles, boots, bindings, and dreams of skiing with Mary Forbes.

We went to the slopes, watched for her hot pink ski parka, and watched to see which lucky stiff would get to ski with her that weekend. Every weekend, it was one of those older guys. You know the type: over the hill, twenty-two, a fancy ski patrol jacket, and an ego bigger than the mountain. We skied all weekend, had a great time, tried to bump into Mary, and usually did a lot more looking than skiing. When the weekend was over, we would be tired on the drive home. We'd talk about the geek who was with Mary. Quietly we each would wish we were over the hill, like the twenty-two-year-old guy with the fancy ski patrol jacket. If we were skiing with Mary, our egos would probably be bigger than the mountain too.

One weekend, we were waiting to get on the T-bar. For those of you who are not skiers, the T-bar is almost exactly what it sounds like. It is a metal bar that's shaped like an upside-down T. It was the lift that pulled us up the mountain, and the pulley system never stops. When it is your turn, you walk in front of it as best as you can walk with skis on, let it hit you in the hind end, and hope the bar doesn't kill you or maim you for life. The way the lines were set up made it the luck of the draw for who would be on the other side of the T.

That day, I hit the lottery. You guessed it. As the lines were going, Mary and I were about to be paired off. I probably could have sold my place to one of the guys for a full tank of gas, an oil change, a wash and wax, and a week of their lunches—all those things that are important to a teenage guy. But no way! Riding with Mary Forbes on the T-bar outweighed any bribe.

When our turn came, I rushed to get in front of the T-bar, crossed the tips of my skis, and almost tripped.

Mary smiled and said, "Hi."

The T-bar pulled us up the hill.

Mary said she had seen me there a lot.

I said, "Yeah, I think I've seen you here before too." I did not want to tell her I had spied on her for six weeks—or that I knew her name, address, telephone number and had snapshots of her in that hot pink parka on my bedroom wall.

She said, "This is the last run of the day for me because I have to go home early. Why don't you call me? My phone number is in the book. If you are coming up next weekend, maybe we can ski together."

I tried not to jump up and down, scream my thanks to the heavens, or act excited in any way. I just said, "Sure. I'll give you a call."

I skied off like I was going down a different trail because I didn't want to mess things up by acting too interested. Besides, the guys were coming up behind me, and I couldn't wait to rub it in, lay it on, or do anything else with the news. After several "Yeah, rights," "You liar," and "You've got to be kidding me," the guys finally believed. For the rest of the day, I was king of the mountain—at least in the eyes of the guys.

The following week seemed to last forever. I wished I could go to sleep and wake up on Saturday morning at 5:30. I spent several hours in front of the mirror with my medicated pads, making sure I didn't break out with a big zit on my forehead. Finally, Saturday morning came.

I had arranged to meet Mary in front of the ski lodge at nine. I got there at eight—just to make sure I didn't miss her: At 8:57, she arrived. Mary wanted to ski the chair that day. It is the same thing as the T-bar except you walk out in front of a moving chair. When it hits you in the hind end, you sit down and up the mountain you start—all in one motion. As we headed up the mountain, I knew I had died and gone to heaven. I didn't remember the pain of getting killed. What I didn't realize was that the pain was about to come.

When we reached the top of the mountain, I was so engrossed in how lucky I was that I would have followed Mary anywhere she wanted to go. The problem arose when I realized where she wanted to. The trail she was headed for—Dead Man's Run—had big expert warnings all around it. I remembered how long Mary had been skiing. What could I do at the age of sixteen? Could I tell her the truth—that I couldn't ski that well and embarrass myself—or just do it and hope for only a broken leg? At age sixteen, I made the decision to die in a skiing accident instead of dying of the embarrassment of chickening out.

Like any gentleman would do, I told Mary to go ahead and that I would follow. I watched her carve her way down the mountain with the skills of an Olympic contender. As I looked down the ninety-degree angle I was about to ski down with two long wooden things strapped to my feet, I wondered how badly it hurt to die. I decided it couldn't be as bad as embarrassing myself in front of Mary or having the guys know I chickened out.

I pushed myself off the edge. I had decided to show off by getting into the tuck position and going for it! As I went past Mary, I am sure I was going a hundred miles per hour. I was totally out of control. I stayed in the tuck position to look like I had everything under control. When I was out of Mary's sight, I began to scream, "Look out! I can't stop! Please, God, I will never do this again if you can save me!"

As luck would have it—or maybe God had a hand in it—I stopped. For the rest of the day, Mary decided to ski the T-bar, which led to easier hills. I still don't know if it was because she knew I was going to kill myself or if she was afraid she couldn't keep up with me!

Our love affair lasted three weeks. Like any good teenage romance, it consisted of several hours on the phone, two more skiing trips, and five kisses.

Thinking back, a question still sticks in my mind. How many times in life are we going to allow our egos to leave us standing all alone at the top of Dead Man's Run?

What Does Love Look Like?

What does love look like? Well, it's black and white with red lips and a blue ribbon around its neck, and it is shaped like a cat. When my son was four, he proved it. He came home one day all excited. He needed three dollars for something he just had to have at a garage sale next door.

He said, "Please, Mommy." And then he was on his way.

Love showed up moments later when he came back with a black and white, red-lipped, wooden cat with a blue ribbon around its neck. He said, "Mommy, I bought this for you!"

Whoever said you can't buy love was wrong. My son bought it for three bucks that day, and my wife still feels that love every time she sees it years later. Love is a language of actions—not words—and we all speak it a little differently.

As life goes on, we learn about love's quiet side. We learn it doesn't have to be some big act or gesture. Watch for it today. It might be the way someone touches your hand or quietly glances at you and smiles. Love has many faces. Sometimes we just don't recognize it because we think we know what it should look like. Let your love be an endless description of something indescribable and wonderful. What does love look like for you?

Shopping with the Twins

My wife forged out to buy a pair of jeans. For most of you, I am sure that doesn't sound like a major undertaking—not like climbing Mount Everest or swimming the English Channel. What I didn't tell you is that she brought the twins with her—the two little bundles of love.

The first trick was to keep one clean while she was dressing the other one. Once this was accomplished, the challenge was to get them moving in the same direction at the same time. Even getting them in the car was a challenge. After getting this done, it was off to the store—or should I say off to the battleground.

On the way there, the boys fought about who was sitting in the front seat, who was sitting in the front seat on the way home, and why they couldn't bring the dog. By this time, most people would begin to wonder if it was worth it. Not my wife. She was determined that two four-year-olds were not going to keep her home. Like any parent about to enter the retail arena with four-year-olds, she began to lay down the law: no running up and down the aisles, no jumping in and out of the clothes racks, and stay right beside me. She included the usual bribe and threat, saying, "If you are good, maybe we can get an ice cream on the way home. If you are not, you are going to go to bed early tonight."

When I tell you what happened next, you will know my wife had no problem deciding whether it was going to be ice cream or early to bed.

The first sign of trouble occurred on the way into the store. Both boys said simultaneously, "I hate this store."

At that point, the boys must have decided that ice cream wasn't worth it. They became as determined not to be there as my wife was determined that two four-year-olds were not going to keep her home. The boys were smart and waited for the right chance. The fact that we live in a very small town and know all the sales clerks in the store gave them the chance they were waiting for. My wife picked out several pairs of jeans to try on and headed for the dressing room.

The sales clerks thought the boys were so cute. Their mistake was when they offered to watch them. The boys stood there like two little angels until Mom closed the door to the dressing room. The click of the door closing was the beginning of the end. The boys made an immediate dive for the circular clothing racks, and the game of hide-and-seek was on. As the clerks looked on, the clothing started to fly. So did the "now, honeys."

A parent who can hear but cannot see what is going on knows that "now, honey" means trouble. The kid is about to do something he or she shouldn't—or more likely, the kid is right in the middle of doing it.

At that point, my wife decided she'd better look to see what "now, honey" the boys were up to. As soon as she opened the door, saw the clerk's face, and saw the clothes flying off the circular rack, she didn't have to guess who was in the middle of it. Times like that test your coping skills. You'd love to scream, but instead, you quietly say, "Get over here." You don't want to embarrass yourself any more than the child already has. Your tone seems to tell the children what you are really thinking, and they respond.

This performance went on about three times, but my wife was determined. The problem was that the boys were too. They decided the usual tricks were not going to get Mom out of the dressing room. They decided they needed a new direction, and they came up with a sure thing to get any parent out of any dressing room anywhere in the United States!

There she was, with her pants down to her knees, when she thought she heard it. The second time, she was sure of it. Yes, the boys had come up with a biggie. In their four-year-old minds, they decided that stress hadn't gotten Mom out of the store, but a massive embarrassment was sure to. They were right. They were running up and down the aisles of the store and screaming, "Penis!" At that point, my wife was questioning her choice of teaching the boys the proper name for it.

She had to make a decision. Should she stay in the dressing room until the store closed and everyone went home? Was quietly leaving the store, bringing them home, and killing them a better idea? She decided to leave the store quietly, take them home, and let them think about it in bed all afternoon.

When I arrived home that evening and heard the story, I decided to check in on the boys. At that point, I realized what a strong woman my wife really was. I discovered that the boys were still breathing, still able to sit down, and still smirking about the look on their mother's face when she came out of the dressing room.

The years have passed, and my wife and I can laugh about it now. When I am older, I am going to ask my dad if he and Mom ever laughed about the little mishap I caused at my mother's annual garden party. I don't think it's quite time to bring it up, but the memory of it makes me not worry so much about the twins and how they are going to turn out. If I turned out okay, there is still a lot of hope for the boys.

The
Zamboni

I came home from work today only to discover I was wrong. The twins and I had been watching the Winter Olympics together on and off for the past week. I thought it was a great experience for the boys to see such wonderful role models and learn about dedication focus, positive thinking, and all that. I thought it was making a real impression on them about goals and achievements.

When my wife and I got home from work, we discovered what had really impressed the boys: the Zamboni! For those of you who missed the Olympics or maybe missed this detail that was so important to my eleven-year-old boys, a Zamboni is a machine that smoothes the ice and was named after its inventor, Frank J. Zamboni. I knew it had impressed the boys so much when I saw the mess in the kitchen and on the front porch. They had turned the neighbor's driveway, much to his dismay, into a skating rink. Their very own handmade Zamboni, which consisted of one sled full of screwdriver holes and several plastic milk cartons with the same screwdriver holes, was on our front porch. The water was leaking out of the holes, onto the sled, through the sled, and onto the front steps. Believe me, the ice was smooth!

After several attempts of trying to get into the house, I started my interrogation like any good parent would do. My teenage daughters had been in charge for the day, but they still had the marks on their heads where the phone had been glued all day. The twins still had the wild look in their eyes all good inventors have—and I still had questions about why I didn't go over the edge. I decided it must have been the swimming pool. What does a swimming pool have to do with the whole thing? Well, one day while my parents were away, my friends and I decided we would dig a swimming pool in the backyard.

I am not talking about a kiddy pool. I am talking about a sixteen-foot-by-thirty-foot pool with room for a slide. Luckily, we had done it in the furthest corner of my parents' lot, which wasn't very developed anyway. Yes, once the initial shock was over, my parents handled it quite well. My mother decided to let us continue.

We were three eleven-year-olds with a dream, a Boy Scout hatchet, my dad's best gardening shovel, and Ricky Spadafore's mother's spade. We worked from sunup to sundown for several weeks and probably still would be digging if it weren't for Bobby Silver. Bobby came over one day and made us an offer we couldn't refuse. We could join his club and hang around the clubhouse all day for twenty-five cents. Now that might not sound too interesting, but what I didn't tell you is that the membership did have its privileges. The one that sold us was that the members of the club could spy on Bobby's older sister and her boyfriend making out on the back porch every night.

The twins had been on vacation for a few days, getting bored, and all they had done was build a Zamboni. When we were kids, we would get out of school for vacation and be bored to death after a few days. Just before it was time to go back to school, we would find some great thing to do all day, such as building a cabin, starting a clubhouse, or finding a neat place to go on a picnic. Just when we stopped being bored, it was time to go back to school.

Looking back on all that made me realize something. I heard the late, great Earl Nightingale refer to the fact he thought life was a vacation on this great big beautiful island we called earth. It scares me a little bit. All the times we go around saying we are bored—and we don't go out and find the fun in life. Are we being like we were as kids on summer vacation? I am not going to wait until just before the vacation is over to start having fun. If you have a swimming pool to dig, someone's older sister to spy on, or a Zamboni to build, what are you waiting for?

Bumper Stickers

I 've always hated bumper stickers. I also hate those little stuffed animals people stick on the windows of their cars. Why do they do that? Let's face it. Cars nowadays cost so much you have to mortgage your children to buy one. The way your children act sometimes can make you feel like not making the car payment. Know what I mean? With this major expense, why would anybody want to put those two-dollar stickers all over it? I think I found one of the reasons, and the story begins with my new car.

I bought a new, red, two-seater, sports car. Have you ever noticed how good a new car looks in your driveway away from all those other new cars? I was quietly trying to hold back my feelings about how cool I was. It was in my driveway, and the neighbors all came over. My friends … well, I went straight to show them. The chrome was polished, and the tires were white and black. I would go out and look at it about every two minutes. The proper name for its color was Rio red, which kind of sounded better than just red. The look of it sitting in my driveway was so cool. It was the kind of car you don't drive while wearing a suit. That baby called for a jean shirt, a red-necked bandanna, and boots.

My seven-year-old son came out and taught me that life is really all about giving. He walked up to me and proudly said, "Daddy, I bought something for your new car!"

I couldn't imagine what a seven-year-old would buy for a Rio-red, two-seater, unbelievably cool sports car. The day before, his grandma had sent him a card with five dollars in it. With all the secrecy of a well-written spy movie, he and his mother had gone to the store on a quest. At that age, I guess certain things are as cool—or I guess as they say now as *awesome*—to a seven-year-old as they are to a thirty-five-year-old. From out from his back, he pulled—yep, you guessed it—one of those stuffed animals for the window of the car and a sticker for the window that read: *Who says I'm off the wall!?!*

I'm sure all the color went out of my face, but I put on a huge smile and said, "This is great!"

What else could I do? My seven-year-old son thought enough of me to spend his own money on something he considered awesome for his dad. Thank God I had the sense to realize the car would come and go—but my seven-year-old thinking that much of me would be more precious than the sports car.

Maybe one of the reasons you see all those animals and stickers on car windows is because that person had a seven-year-old who loved them too.

The years have passed, and the Rio-red sports car has turned orange from the sun. The teddy bear is still in the window, but he is more beige than brown. I have learned something. All of us with children have worn (just to make them feel good) a popcorn necklace or a big carnation made out of orange construction paper that one of our loves has made in school. We get into our cars, and on the way to our destinations, off comes the necklace or the carnation so we don't embarrass ourselves. Maybe we should leave them on and not be embarrassed. Maybe we should be proud and wear them like a sign that says, "I'm a parent, and they love me." Whoever said you don't get medals for being parents was wrong. I keep mine in the window of my Rio-red two-seater sports car.

The Blessed Tree

My twins went into the woods to find a Christmas tree. What they came out with was a miracle.

Christmas was only three weeks away when the story began. The stores were all packed with shoppers who were hurrying about their business with not enough time in the day. The school plays were all scheduled. East Central High was going to do another rendition of "The Three Wise Men Meet Santa Claus." People's Christmas lists were bigger than their bank accounts. But that didn't matter. All the stores were advertising no money down and no payments until June. Yes, it looked like it was going to be a typical Christmas in Small Town, USA—until the Friday night my twelve-year-old twins asked their mother for permission to go into the woods and cut down their own Christmas tree for their room. We had just moved to the country that year, and the boys had a room the size of a small house. She gave them permission, and they went off to bed.

When we came downstairs the next morning, much to our surprise, there was a note on the kitchen table. The boys had already left on their quest to find the perfect tree. The note was written in red crayon on a blank sheet of white paper:

> Mom, we went to get our tree.
> Love, Bryan and Brent

My wife and I looked at each other and thought about how cute it was that they were excited enough to leave so early in the morning. I headed off to work, my went wife to the barn, and our day had begun. It When my wife came out of the barn and saw the sight she did, she knew our Christmas was about to change.

She heard a noise and looked up at the hill. She saw the boys coming from a distance. One was pulling a hot purple plastic sled across the fresh blanket of white snow, and the other was pulling a skinny, little pine tree. All she could do was smile as she watched them come closer and closer, all dressed in their oversized boots, scarves, and winter hats, bringing home their prize tree.

When they got closer, she could see they had red faces, runny noses, and a story to tell. On the purple sled, they had the weapons they had taken into the woods to bring down their first Christmas tree. They consisted of two dull axes, one rusty hacksaw, and a hammer that was never supposed to leave the barn.

When they got to her, they were out of breath. With their eyes the size of saucers, they said, "Mommy, you won't believe what happened!"

When they caught their breath, they told her how they looked and looked but couldn't find any Christmas trees. When they were about to give up, they came across a tree growing out of a stump. After they argued about whether or not it was going to be their tree, they decided they would take it as their special tree.

They got their tools ready, and when the saw blade touched the tree, the clouds opened up and a ray of sun came upon their tree. It was so bright that it blinded them for a moment. They felt this feeling all through them. They said it was like a TV show. They expected the angels to start singing. Neither of them spoke a word as they cut down the tree, but as they were walking home, they decided they didn't care if they came across a tree that looked like it came off a Christmas tree lot—they knew that this one was theirs.

My wife canceled her plans for the day. Instead, she went to the cellar with the boys and found the perfect Christmas decorations for the little pine tree. They went out and bought a special string of lights for it. They set it up in their room, and the boys wanted to put a little manger scene under it that had been their grandma's.

My wife stepped back from the tree when it was all done and said, "There. It's perfect!"

The boys said, "We know. Someone perfect picked it out for us." The boys talked about Baby Jesus a little more that year. I called their skinny little tree "the blessed tree."

A few days later, I was sitting at the kitchen table with one of the boys. It was a cloudy day, and in the distance, we saw a bright ray of sun coming out of the clouds.

He turned to me and said, "Maybe someone else is picking out a Christmas tree."

I just smiled and said, "Maybe."

I think God touched the boys with that little tree. I know He touched me. I would go up in their room to check on them every night before I went to bed and turn the lights out on "the blessed tree." I would look at them in the soft light and then at the tree. I would look up and say, "Thank you."

Christmas came and went. After the holidays passed, I went out into the garage and saw "the blessed tree" waiting to be thrown out and taken to the dump. Something told me I couldn't let that happen.

I went back into the house and told my wife I was bringing "the blessed tree" back where it came from. There was a blizzard that day, and it was getting dark. Everyone thought I was nuts for going out there, especially at that time of day, but I knew I had to bring "the blessed tree" back into the woods—back to where God had given it to the boys.

The snow was deep. I frantically looked for the right spot as daylight faded. Right when I was about to find "the blessed tree" stump, something told me most of us give up right before we are about to succeed. I said, "Come on, blessed tree, where are you?" I turned, and right there before me, I saw the stump. I duct taped the "blessed tree" back together, took off my hat, held it to my chest, and stood in silent reverence for a moment. I closed my eyes and said a prayer of thanks to God for the tree.

As I walked home, I felt good about what I had done. The snow and wind had stopped. A feeling of peace came over me. I came to the top of the hill and saw our house. The sun was just disappearing into the night, leaving a beautiful red glow in the sky. It seemed to finish the day off at peace. I realized I was a little different for doing something like that, but that's what my wife says she likes about me. I don't know if the tree will ever grow again, but I knew I just couldn't throw it out to the road.

My wife said, Maybe a seed will fall from it, and there will be more 'blessed trees' for other little children to find."

Maybe a red-faced, runny-nosed child with a story to tell will look up at the prized tree with eyes like saucers and say, "Grandpa, you won't believe what happened!" Dad will look over at them and smile, and we will both turn to the child and say, "Oh, yes, honey. We believe. We believe."

The Grasshopper Suit

My fifteen-year-old gave me a lesson in mathematics today. Take two pipe cleaners, one hooded sweatshirt, two pieces of green construction paper, one ball of green twine, one jar of sparkles, and two round brass paper fasteners and what do you get? The answer is *love*—and that I am sure of.

We were going through some old pictures today with his grandma when we ran across a picture of him in his famous grasshopper suit with operational grasshopper legs and wings. He started to tell his grandma the story about the suit. I noticed a change come over him as he began to speak louder and faster. It was a look of excitement as he boasted how Brenda had stayed up all night to make the suit for him. He said, "It was the best suit ever. The legs really moved. All the other kids' bug suits looked like something you would find on our windshields."

As I listened to him talk, I looked down at the picture and then back at him. When he said Brenda's name, I saw a little twinkle in his eye. I remembered how the famous grasshopper suit with the operational grasshopper legs and wings came to be.

He was in the fourth grade, and he was going to be in a play to celebrate the importance of bugs in our lives. He needed a bug costume. He came to stay with us for a weekly visit and happened to tell us how he needed the outfit in two days. Everyone he asked had told him they had no idea how to make a bug costume. So he guessed he would just have to put on a garbage bag, draw some whiskers on his face, and be a "whatever."

Brenda could see the disappointment in his face and volunteered to take on the task that no one else seemed to want. I remember the look on his face when he first tried on the costume. It was the same look he had when he told Grandma about the famous grasshopper suit.

As Jason retold the story, he jumped for joy—just as he did the day he jumped across the stage in fourth grade with his famous grasshopper suit.

I am not sure how far a grasshopper can jump, but I am sure no grasshopper has ever jumped so proudly or felt so loved.

The play was supposed to be about the importance of bugs in our lives, but the lesson I learned from the play was the importance of the little things in life.

I think we all have special memories of something someone did for us. The special little moment can't be explained, but the joy of it can always be felt by thinking about it. I saw that in my fifteen-year-old. For me, it was back in the fifties on a warm July day when Mom came in and got me up from a nap. She held me in her arms as we sat on the front porch and watched the Fourth of July parade. Thanks, Mom. I know that moment wasn't about the parade; it was just one of those unexplainable moments. Thank God.

I am sure a grasshopper suit and a parade can add up to love. What is the equation in your life?

Notes from Home

A 2½-inch rectangular piece of paper brought my son through a time in his life when he was searching for who he was, but the story really began years earlier.

When my son was in high school, I would write a note every morning and put it in his lunch with a saying or a drawing. Some were funny, and some were deep. His friends all got to the point where they wanted to hear the note for that day. If I missed putting one in, I heard about it.

When I wrote the notes, they would just come to me. I would sometimes just scribble on a piece of paper and make something funny out of it. The deep ones included:

> *If you are ever down and begin to wonder if there is a God, watch a sunset, listen to a bird sing, ask for help, and watch it come.*

> *Sometimes something that does not look like much, when studied, becomes a beautiful thing.*

> *Take time to appreciate nature; it's the way God decorated our home.*

> *Just call me lucky because that's what I call myself when I think about you.*

The kindest thing you can do for yourself today is give away your love to someone in a smile, a touch, a word, or a selfless act of kindness.

When he graduated and was going off to college, I decided to continue the notes. I couldn't actually write them every morning. I needed to write a lot of them, and my wife joined in the writing. When we looked for something special to put them in, I knew right where to go.

Grandma Spear would have something. She was in her eighties and collected antiques for years. I wanted something that would last—something that was magical—and that's what we found. It was almost like it was meant to be. It was a special antique cookie tin that had been waiting for years to be chosen to hold the love that would now be in that can. The three angels on the cover had been tattered over the years. When I picked it up, a beautiful feeling went through my body. I knew he would be all right. Someone was looking over him, and the notes would guide him.

He came home for Thanksgiving that year, and one day, I went up in his room and opened the can. I wanted to remember some of the notes. In the can, I found a note he had put inside. He was asking God to help him. I am not sure what he was going through at the time, but I am happy and thankful God helped him in his search.

A note he loved said, "You make me as proud as a peacock with his tail feathers fanned." Just a week ago, I found a picture of a peacock and sent it to him with a note that said, "I thought of you today." Even though he is a grown man now with a life of his own, I know he smiled that day.

If you have notes in your life you'd like to send home, just take a 2½-inch rectangular piece of paper and let your heart speak. Let your artistic flair come out. If you run into a tattered antique cookie tin with three angels on it, you will be blessed—and love will open your heart.

Mama

Grandma called today with a special request. What she asked for made me proud, sad, and determined. She asked me to write something about her and my mom to be read at her funeral. Mom died this past December after six months of fighting brain cancer. I think Grandma died a little too. Mom was her only child. I watched the way she cared for Mom. As time went on, Mom regressed, and Grandma traveled back in time with her.

I learned one of the greatest lessons of my life while watching the two of them. I had a forty-five-minute drive to see Mom, and I tried to make it every day. One particular day, I was driving and thinking about how I could go there, get everyone gathered around Mom, hold hands, and lead a prayer. I had my Christian music blasting in the car, and by God, I knew I could perform a miracle. At times like that, we are brought back to our beliefs in faith. That is when God takes the opportunity to show us the right way, and that day was no different.

I walked into the house with all the mighty intentions of taking over and performing the ultimate healing. It was going to be the greatest show of love ever! The surprise was that when I walked in, the greatest show of love was already happening. Frail and suffering from myasthenia gravis, which is a disease that affects sight and balance, my eighty-four-year old grandmother stood beside my mom, her baby. Quietly, without fanfare, and with no audience to applaud, there she was. As always, Grandpa was sitting at the head of the bed.

At two o'clock every afternoon, even when Mom was in a deep coma, Grandma would fix each of them a cup of tea. Sometimes Mom would drink a sip with much help from Grandma. Mom chose not to be fed intravenously, and Grandma knew that she had to get fluids into her to keep her alive. I watched the love as Grandma quietly talked baby talk to her little girl—and Grandpa sat quietly by their sides.

I sat down and thought of my children. I was lucky to have five of them, and I sometimes didn't appreciate them enough. I watched the courage and love of these two old people watching their only baby die before them. It wasn't supposed to be that way. How foolish I had been earlier with my big ideas! I thought about how many times in life we do nothing to love or help others because we think it has to be some grand act. Well, that day, I saw real love: giving of yourself to another. The act doesn't have to be large. My grandma did it with her cup of tea.

I cried all the way home that day. Maybe it was because I felt badly for my grandparents, maybe my mom, or maybe it was because I had been shown a lesson that I didn't want to see. It is easier in life to have big plans to love than to take the small steps of doing it. I had the chance to do that with my mom before she died. I would go down there and read my poems about life.

She would smile, amazed by the depth of my thoughts, and say, "When did you grow up? You are not a little boy anymore."

I was thirty-eight years old, but the kind of growing up she was talking was in my thoughts. I was very lucky to have had that time with Mom. Her little boy had finally grown up.

When she died, I found out she had asked to have some of my writings read at her funeral. It was one of the greatest honors I will ever receive in my life.

Grandma has given me another honor with her request. The only thing I am sure I will write is that my mother still called her mother "Mama" at age fifty-nine. It always amazed me. Now I realize why. Mama is one of the most endearing words in the English language. Grandma Spear fits the description of someone who would be called Mama.

I will probably talk about the things they did together and the way they treated each other. And the ending will go something like this:

Yes, Mom and Grandma had a special love. None of us is sure what happens in the end. The only thing I am sure of is that if they are ever together again, she'll still call her "Mama."

If you have some grand plan in life about how you are going to help mankind, great! In the meantime, why don't you just smile at a stranger today or take a loved one out for tea at two o'clock?

Fire in
the Sky

At 8:15 in the morning, my mother's life on earth ended. I had taken the kids to school that morning when my wife received the news. As I entered the house, the look on her face, the compassion of her hug, and the words she spoke ("I am sorry") said it all. Mom was gone. She had been fighting brain cancer for six months, and the battle reached an end that morning.

As I watched Mom fade over the last months of her life, I thought I was dealing with her death and was ready for it. But that morning, with the blow to my heart, I realized that I had never been ready. At times, as she suffered, I wished for her death so her suffering would be over. Every time I wished this, I felt guilty for having had such a thought.

It wasn't until that morning, however, that I realized I logically knew she was dying. It was happening right in front of me, yet someplace in my heart, I didn't want to accept it. I wanted to have her for one more day, one more moment, and have one more chance to hold her hand, touch her face, and tell her I loved her. I never got that chance because we lived thirty-five miles away, and I didn't get there in time. I so wished I could have. She was my mother; she couldn't leave me.

I really needed to know if she was with God and if she was okay. I wasn't so sure about what I had always professed to believe. I had always believed that when death on earth occurred, we went home to Jesus if we had accepted Him as our Savior. After all, when Jesus talked to the believing criminal on the cross next to him he said, "Today you will be with me in paradise. This is a solemn promise" (Luke 23:43). However, this was no criminal we were talking about here. It was my mother, and I wanted some proof.

Just a few weeks earlier, I had been driving home one night late from work. I had, as I thought at that time, a major decision to make in my life. I asked God to show me a sign if the decision I was leaning toward was the right one. At that very moment, a shooting star streaked across the sky—not up or down—just straight across in front of me. I knew, trusted, and believed that it was my sign.

With the news of my mother's death, I found myself again needing to see, believe, and have proof that my mother was safe with Jesus. My entire belief system had been rocked. Knowing God could do shooting stars, I asked for another one to give me proof Mom was with Him.

The rest of the day was filled with the pain and the busy tasks of a wake. We picked the children up from school, and they knew without a spoken word that their grandma had died. Our faces could not hide our grief or conceal the pain we felt for our children. We had a forty-five-minute journey to my parents' home where the family was gathering with Dad.

The next three days were full of family, friends, memories, laughter, and tears. On the third day, my mother's funeral service took place, and it was the longest morning of my life. I felt the sorrow of saying good-bye and watched my family suffer the same emotions. That afternoon, the family went back to Dad's house.

That evening, we put away the dinner dishes, hugged, and said much we loved each other. It was time for us to start our drive home. It was getting late, and we were all physically and emotionally exhausted. The children fell asleep in the car, and I just enjoyed the quiet time after three days of the funeral process. It seemed good to be alone and silent with my thoughts.

Suddenly, a voice in my head said, "Remember the shooting star."

I had forgotten all about it during the stress and busyness of the past three days. I looked to the sky, fully expecting to see the shooting star. As I looked up, I scanned the most overcast winter sky I had ever seen. The clouds fully masked any chance of seeing a shooting star. At first, I felt disappointment because I knew it wouldn't mean anything if I didn't see my shooting star during the three-day wake period. After all, I would see other shooting stars in my lifetime.

Realizing I wouldn't see a shooting star that night, I decided to trust that Mom was with God. I knew she was okay. He had never let me down before. When I let go of needing Him to prove it to me, the second I trusted Him in my heart, a ball of fire the size of a basketball came shooting out of the sky.

It was so bright that it woke up my wife. She said, "What was that? What was that?"

Through tears of joy, I replied, "That was my sign. That was my sign."

As I drove the rest of the way home, I knew I had been blessed because I had done what Jesus spoke of in John 20:29. He said, "Blessed are those who have not seen and yet have believed."

I also understood why Mom always said, "When you give for the right reasons, it comes back to you tenfold."

I gave up a little shooting star that night and was given back fire in the sky.

Titanic

My wife and I went to see James Cameron's *Titanic*. He added a beautiful love story to the tragedy, and the hero and heroine risked everything to be together until the end. It made me think about how many real, untold love stories there must have been that terrible night. Part of the tragedy is that those stories will never be told.

Stories of love lift our spirits and allow us to believe in love, which gives us courage, hope, and the will to endure. My wife reached over and held my hand during the movie. Without a word being spoken, I think we became a little closer. We both knew that if we were on that ship that night, we would have stayed together until the end. I looked over at her and saw a tear roll down her face, and I kissed it away. I wonder what really happened that dreadful night.

When we got home and went to bed, we held each other a little tighter. As I wrote this story, tears rolled down my face at the thought of the lives lost, the lovers separated, and the hopes and dreams that were never to be realized. I'd like to think the lives lost will remind us to live our lives to the fullest. I also like to think that God brought them all home that night.

I told my wife once, that if I died before her, and got to heaven and she wasn't there it wouldn't be heaven. I am hopeful though Einstein said that all time is *now*, and they say that eternity is but a blink of an eye on earth. I wouldn't have to wait for her long, but if that's not what happens, I will just pull up a chair, wait at the gates, close my eyes, and see her in all the things I have ever loved.

Love stories are not only for the movies. Live yours to the fullest, and most of all, don't forget to play your part as if your whole life's happiness depends on it—because it does. Places, everyone. Quiet on the set. Action!

Kindred
Spirits

I think the most unforgettable moments in our lives can start years earlier. This story is one of those moments.

Four years ago, two ladies walked into my store. They were looking for a very special gift—a gift from their hearts. They were looking for a Pandora bracelet and wanted to put an "angel of hope" charm on it. They told me how one of their daughters-in-law had been pregnant with twins, but she had miscarried and lost both babies. They wanted to give her this angel to represent the babies and give her some peace.

When I heard the story, I felt such compassion for them and the young woman I'd never met. They didn't know I had twins who were born healthy, normal, and beautiful. I couldn't imagine what it was like for this expectant mom and her family. I so badly wanted to help them in some way. I went to the Pandora case, but we were sold out of angels. I looked through the layaways, but there was no angel to be found. Then I had an idea. I asked the women to come back in an hour because I thought I knew where I might find one. They agreed to come back.

I immediately went home. I started to cry as I told my wife the story of what had happened.

When I was done, Brenda took off her bracelet and began to remove the charms until she came to her angel of hope charm. As she handed the charm to me, she said, "We have our boys, our angels. This angel belongs to her. Tell them I will never put another angel on my bracelet in honor of her."

I returned to the store. I don't know why I didn't tell them where I got the angel, but I didn't. I just gave them the angel and refused to charge them for it. They thanked me over and over again and then left the store. Weeks later, they came back and told me how much the charm meant to the young woman. She loved her special gift. We talked for a while, and I ended up telling them the whole story.

Years have passed since then, and the story came full circle this week. Brenda was at the dentist in a nearby town. As she entered the room, the dental hygienist said, "I love your bracelet." She looked down at the paperwork again and said, "Are you Carbino's Jewelry Store?"

Brenda said, "Yes, I am."

The young lady now had tears in her eyes. "You are going to make me cry."

Brenda asked, "Why?"

The young lady reached for the bracelet on her wrist and turned it over gently. With two fingers, she held up the "angel of hope" charm and said, "This is your angel."

Brenda said, "You are the girl who lost the twins?"

The woman said, "Yes, I am."

The two hugged each other and cried. Two strangers were touched by an act of kindness and by a sterling silver angel that was much more to both of them than just a charm. The two women had become kindred spirits. They were two moms who understood a mother's love.

The young woman told my wife the story of the day she received the "angel of hope" charm. It had been a few months since she lost the twins, and she was afraid to hope again. But the day she got the bracelet, she felt like taking a second chance at hope. The day she received her charm she went to the store and bought a pregnancy test, and it was positive. She then showed Brenda a picture of her beautiful, healthy, three-year-old baby girl she was pregnant with the day the 'angel of hope' came. The two strangers hugged and cried together again: happy tears, tears of thankfulness, and tears of hope.

Scottie

On the day I was to meet her, the arrangements were all set. All I knew about her was her name, her age, the color of her hair, and that she was coming to a friend's house that day. We would meet at last.

I got up that morning, and the excitement mounted. I couldn't stand still. Thoughts raced through my head. What would she look like? What would her personality be like? How would we hit it off? Then it happened. The phone rang, and she had arrived to meet me. Would I say the right things? Would I act the right way? Would she like me? Would we be good for each other?

My mind was racing so fast as I drove in the driveway that I just missed the mailbox and the birdbath. I turned and spotted her in the distance. She took my breath away. The wind lightly blew her auburn hair. Even from a distance, I could see the warmth in her eyes. I walked toward her, and as her eyes met mine, I was consumed by the moment. I drew her into me, and before I spoke a word, I breathed into her nose. She whinnied, and I knew I was in love. Scottie, my horse, was finally here.

The way I described Scottie probably would give away to any horse person the fact that I didn't know a lot about horses. They are absolutely right. When I first got Scottie, I thought the horse's gait was the fence it went through to get into the barn. I still can't figure out why the proper name for its hair is a coat—it's not like it has buttons. The first time they told me to put a halter on her, I thought, *You have got to be kidding! A tube top would be much easier.*

I was the proud owner of a horse, but there was a catch. Scottie was given to me because she had been abused almost to the point of death. I volunteered to rehabilitate her. The way I described her when I met her is the way I saw her. The description was far from reality. She was two hundred pounds underweight. Her face, legs, chest, and stomach were raw from having been left unattended without shelter. The black flies had almost literally eaten her alive. Her wounds were running, open sores. Her back and body were crooked from her hooves not being taken care of for months. She was in such pain that she had to hold one leg up all the time, but all I could see was the warmth in her eyes, the gentleness in her face, and the quiet way her look asked for help. That day, I decided I would do anything I could to help her.

My wife already owned a horse and had been influential in my getting Scottie. She cried for three days and worried Scottie would die. The lady's farm where we kept Scottie and the person responsible for connecting me with Scottie said she was worse than what she had thought. Scottie was totally unsound, but if I would do the work, she would teach me how to rehabilitate her. Since I knew nothing about horses, I kept saying that she would be okay.

When we began, I couldn't figure out why everyone was so upset. I had no doubt Scottie would be all right. First, we tended to her sores and put her on a balanced diet. The hair she had left was so bleached by the sun that it was falling out. I shampooed her almost every day with a medicated shampoo. I kept the cosmetic companies in business that summer by buying body oils, which I watered down, and keeping her greased from head to hoof.

Before work, during my lunch hour, and after supper, I would walk Scottie through poles we placed on the ground in patterns to start building her muscles. At first, I would do it with no weight on her back, but as she grew stronger, I put a saddle on her.

The weeks passed—and the progress was slow—but I knew she would be okay. My whole family got involved. The kids loved and babied her. My wife took turns walking her through the poles in the hot sun. Finally, I started with my smallest child and walked her through the poles with him on her back. As she grew stronger, I put a heavier child on her back. After months, it was my turn to ride. Time has passed, and Scottie can walk, trot, and canter with a rider. The people at the farm who know about horses never thought she would be able to be ridden.

My family gave a lot to Scottie, but she taught me one of the greatest lessons I think I will ever learn. When I got Scottie, my ignorance about horses allowed me to believe she would be okay. If I had understood that it was almost impossible for her to ever get better again, perhaps I would have given up on those hot summer days when I was walking through the poles. Maybe I would have given up and been happy just to have her walk.

I didn't give up because I believed—and that has taught me something you should know. Whenever we go into a circumstance, what we believe is going to happen will happen. If you believe you can do something, you will. If you believe you can't, you might as well give up in the beginning.

By the way, last Sunday afternoon, Scottie and I jumped our first jump together and never touched the bar. If you believe, you can begin to jump over some of the obstacles in your life.

Kids Nowadays

Most of us have heard or said, "Kids nowadays! What's the world coming to?"

In our small community, Brian died at age eighteen of Hodgkin's disease. We saw the pain of losing a friend transform, for a moment, our teenagers into the adults they will become before their years as they said good-bye to a friend. We need not worry about the world anymore.

I watched my seventeen-year-old boys and their friends cry over the loss of Brian and stand silently in line for more than two hours to pay their respects. They all did it with such class and caring, and it made me proud.

The school choir sang the "Wind Beneath My Wings" at the funeral, and the soccer team and the school band stood at attention with a grace and dignity I don't think I could have had. They held each other and fixed each other's ties as they wiped tears away from each other's eyes. In some way, they made it into a beautiful tribute to Brian that he would have been proud of. They set him free that day. Somehow they knew that love never dies—it just changes form.

Brian is with us now. You'll feel him in a soft breeze that cools a hot summer night, a smile from a stranger that just feels different, or a shooting star that lights up the night for a single second. You will know him in your thoughts and in the peace that passes all understanding. It will hold you up and allow you to remember to love and live. God is the love that keeps us strong and allows us to go on.

If your teenager comes running through the kitchen tonight with purple hair, put your arms around him or her for a minute and say, "I love you. You make me proud." If you do that, they will. The Brians who have left this world too soon will look down and say, "We made them see—and they did."

To Brian Patrick Kelly, who could bring out the best qualities of kids nowadays.

Helping Each Other Home

Her name was Karley. We never had a chance to speak to each other. But somehow God brought us together in a place where words didn't matter.

I first heard of Karley when a friend asked us to pray for this precious little four-year-old girl who was dying. Karley was supposed to go to Disney World with the Make-A-Wish Foundation. However, her blood levels needed to go up for her to make the trip. They asked me to help them because I had helped others. Thank God that her blood levels went up—and she was able to make her trip.

A few weeks later, I got a second call. At four o'clock, my friend called me at work to ask if I would drive to Boston Children's Hospital, which was a seven-hour drive away. Karley was dying. I was on my way by 4:30. I drove there that night and prayed for Karley the whole way.

By the time I got there, it was the middle of the night. I drove to the hospital as soon as I got to town. I wondered how I would get into the hospital and into intensive care in the middle of the night. I just walked in and told the guards I was going up to intensive care. They stared blankly and let me in with no questions.

As I walked though the hospital, I kept saying, "I can do all things through Jesus Christ who strengthens me."

When I got upstairs, a nurse told me Karley's family had just left to get a couple hours of sleep. I stayed there a while, prayed for Karley, and sent her all my energy. I could see through the glass windows into her room. It was the first time I saw her. She was a beautiful little baby. I think God was readying her for her trip home. I was just a bystander of a beautiful passing.

I left the hospital at three in the morning and got a hotel room. I slept for a couple hours and went back to the hospital.

In the morning, I spoke with her family and prayed with them. God gave me the act of love he wanted me to do. Her grandmother sat with me, and I tried to comfort her in her sorrow as her parents said good-bye to their baby upstairs. It was getting late when God told me to give the grandmother my Bible so she could read the scripture to Karley before she was gone:

> "But they that wait upon the Lord shall renew their strength. They shall mount up with wings like eagles; they shall run and not be weary; they shall walk and not faint." Isaiah 40:30

I knew it was time for me to go home to my family. I had another seven-hour trip home. I made the night before with very little sleep. As I drove away, I felt some kind of peace. I decided to take the ferry across Lake Champlain that night. The night sky over the water was unbelievable. It looked like there were a million stars on the black velvet sky. I got out of my car, stood on the ferry, and took in the peace, the beauty, and the wonder of God. There were so many shooting stars that night. I will never forget it.

For Karley, I would like to think it was a welcome home with fireworks and all. That's how I will forever hold it in my heart. When we were across the water, I got back in my car and still had a few hours to drive. I was so tired, but I kept driving.

As I got closer to home, I realized there was no way I was going to make it. I tried turning up the radio, opening all the windows, and blasting the air conditioning, but I couldn't stay awake. I called my wife and told her I was going to have to get a hotel. I was only about forty-five minutes away from home. That's when the miracle happened. All at once, I felt this energy like I had never felt before come through me. It was like God sent an angel to bring me home. I was instantly wide-awake, and all my strength came back into me. I will believe and know the rest of my life that Karley and I helped each other home that night. Thank you, Karley. Thank you, God.

Rainbows over Redbrick

My wife and I started a therapeutic horseback-riding center years ago for handicapped children. We had twelve horses and lots of volunteers. The horses were angels. My wife and I had full-time jobs and five teenagers. We were probably a little nuts, but we felt in our hearts that God wanted us to do it.

The first year, we only had a couple riders. My wife told us they would be bringing in busloads. The kids and I laughed and said, "Yeah, right."

A year later, I looked down our long driveway, and tears started to well up in my eyes. A brand-spanking-new school bus was coming to our farm. *My God, they are bringing them in by the busloads,* I thought.

We had lessons every day—and sometimes two. Thank God for the volunteers. It was one of the best times in our lives, and it was also one of the hardest. By the end of the summer, we were so tired. At the end of the day, we would say, "Why are we doing this?"

A day or two later, we would walk out of the barn after another long day and see a double rainbow in front of our property. We would look at each other, smile, and say, "Yeah. That is why we are doing it."

This happened every summer for twelve years. I think God was giving us strength and telling us to keep moving forward. At one time, we had more than three hundred kids coming during the summer. At the end of the lessons, would have little races up and back in the riding ring. On the side, walkers led the horses, and the kids loved it. One lady who came to ride couldn't speak. As we raced down the riding ring, she raised both arms up to the sky and yelled, "I am riding a cow!" In her world, she was riding a cow—and she did it wonderfully. Thank you, God, for moments like that. There were so many.

People still come up to me and say, "I rode horses at your farm."

The fact that they have grown up does matter. I still see the twinkle in their eyes I saw when they were riding at Redbrick. But like all good things, sometimes it must end. The volunteers began to fade away to other things in their lives. It was hard to keep things going financially. Everyone's lives were changing. The economy in our town took quite a hit. We could no longer afford to run our program. We always said we would stop if we could not give the kids the best we had. It was so hard, and those horses had given so much.

In twelve years, we never had an accident. I believe they were angels. How could we just walk away from them? We made one of the hardest decisions we have ever had to make. We would have to find good homes for the horses and give them away. My wife and I cried as we discussed our plans. We didn't sleep half the night.

Early in the morning, our daughter yelled, "Mom, come quick. You have to see this." A double rainbow was engulfing our whole property behind the barn. In the twenty-two years since that beautiful morning, we have not seen another double rainbow behind the barn. It was a special gift for us. We took it as God saying, "Thank you. You did a good job. Redbrick is behind you now." That gave us such peace in the decisions we had to make.

I thank God for that time in our lives—and for all the people who were touched. God gave us the strength to carry out our mission, and He gave us the strength when it was time for it to end. It was a blessed thing.

Midlife Crisis

A thought came to me the other night as I was sitting in my kitchen with my wife, a good friend, and a pot of coffee. We were solving all the world's problems. I decided the real meaning of a midlife crisis. A midlife crisis is when you realize it's halftime in the game of life—and you are not sure you are playing the right position. Sometimes I'm not even sure if I'm in the right game! We all had a laugh over this description and then went on to other subjects. I, however, could not get the midlife crisis thought out of my mind.

I weighed all the issues about this time in a person's life and decided that maybe a midlife crisis is not like society sees it: as a time people go a little crazy. Maybe it's a time when people finally get a little smart. Think about some of the things people do during this time. The people I am talking about are the ones who suddenly change jobs, move away, or just start saying, "What the heck?" Maybe they say, "I've been doing this job I don't like all these years. All I ever do is work." Maybe they realize what they've been doing all their lives doesn't mean anything. Maybe these folks say, "I'm going to take the rest of my life to do what I really enjoy—and do what I dream about." Maybe these people say, "I'm finally going to go for it."

Maybe they realize in the game of life, in their games, they are quarterbacks. Maybe these people have come to the realization that I came to that night in the kitchen. How much more time do I really have? How much more of it will I waste dreaming dreams that can only come true if I stop dreaming and start doing?

Most of us have dreams we are going to accomplish when we have the time. We are too busy serving life instead of living it. During midlife crises, people realize that if they are ever going to play the piano at Carnegie Hall, they better start taking piano lessons.

When I thought more about life, another thought came to me. As teens, most of us know all the answers and are blinded by hormones. In our twenties, we start to see that maybe we still have a little bit more to learn, but it doesn't matter because we have so much time left. In our thirties, we begin to realize that life isn't that long. The people who told us that the years just slip by when you get older were right. They all say life begins at forty, and I am beginning to believe what they all say—whoever they are.

I've watched people who seem to excel. I wondered what drives famous people. *They must have something I don't have. How can I teach my children to have it?* The good news is that after years of wondering, five children, and one midlife crisis, I now know what they have—and I know why life begins at forty for most of us. They have what I call "midlifing-for-life syndrome." This condition of asking yourself the right questions each day that will give you the life you've always wanted. Most of us don't realize the right questions until we reach the middle of our lives, and some of us never know them. I will share with you what I think the right questions are:

- Does what I am doing really mean anything to me and the people I love?
- Does what I'm doing lead me toward what I really want in life—or is it holding me back?
- Is my dream worth spending the time to develop the skills I need to accomplish it? Are there other ways I would like to spend my time that I am not willing to give up for a dream?
- Are my dreams what I think I should want? Do they give me inner peace and fulfillment?
- Am I holding back from going after my dreams because of fear of failure? Am I afraid that if I reach the dream, the rewards won't be as sweet as the expectations?

With all this in mind, I wondered if a midlife crisis should be called an awakening. Some people say life begins at forty. I say life begins when you start asking yourself the right questions. Stop taking yourself so seriously; every once in a while, say, "What the heck?"

Golfing
with God

I went golfing with God and three of my buddies one day. I invited God; the other guys didn't know He was coming. The Holy Ghost was busy, and you have to watch Him because He is invisible, which gives him an advantage (not that we would think He was cheating).

When the boys saw how I was playing, they knew something divine was happening. Paul and Peter where in the rough a lot, but I am sure they didn't give themselves better lies. I swear I saw a little red guy with horns on Peter's shoulder, and I swear I heard the little guy swear.

Everything was going great until Jesus showed up. On the tenth hole, he hit one in the water. None of us complained when he walked on water to get it. We decided we were going to make that one a gimme.

It was a little windy that day, and when I looked over at the lake, I swear the water parted. We didn't mention that to anyone. I figured God must like golf. I hardly ever play golf, and it shows. I asked God for help. I wasn't sure how I was supposed to hold my legs or hands or how to place my feet. I knew I was supposed to keep my head down. I promised God I would do that part if He would help me with the rest.

I stayed focused. I did my part, and God did his. In nine holes, I went from shooting a sixty-three to shooting a forty-seven. The things that happened on the course that day were unbelievable.

I later realized the true lesson of the day. If we do what we know is right in any endeavor and do our parts, God will help with the rest. We must believe and stay focused. We must do our parts.

By the way, on the nineteenth hole, the guy with the long hair that glows has to be the nicest guy ever—and his homemade wine was delicious.

Have Tos
versus
Choose Tos

Thirty seconds after I woke up this morning, I knew it was going to be a good day. I realized I wasn't in the hospital, needed no medical attention, and had all my senses. Nothing happened the night before to make me believe I would be in the hospital, require medical attention, or lose any of my senses. No, that was the way I decided to feel every morning.

The best way to enjoy good health is to visit the hospital once a day. When a family member or friend is in the hospital, we sit in waiting rooms, eat in cafeterias, and wait for the visiting hours to begin and end. We are thankful we are not in there—no matter who the person is. Even for the most powerful person in the world, they don't make gold-lined hospital gowns.

I'm sure that's what Fred Bowman was thinking during his recent hospital stay. Fred had four big problems: his demanding attitude, his two broken legs, the hospital's no-smoking policy, and Fred's four-pack-a-day habit. Fred's wife only had two problems: Fred and how to get Fred out for a few cigarettes. One thing led to another, but when all was said and done, Fred was out on the hospital sidewalk, on a stretcher, in the dead of winter, chain-smoking, and trying to get his quota of nicotine in him. He did pretty well until the nurses realized that Fred was still smoking, but his IV had frozen. Fred was wheeled back into his room. I bet the freedom we enjoy each day to come and go as we please is something Fred learned to appreciate during his hospital stay.

As far as sleeping in a hospital, no matter where you live, it's nice to wake up in your own bed. You don't miss having someone waking you up every forty-five minutes, shining a flashlight in your eyes, sticking a thermometer in your mouth, and telling you to take a deep breath all at the same time.

Then there is the act of going to the bathroom. You either can't get up and some nurse you have never seen before, hopefully, has to slip a cold metal object under your private parts. With this embarrassment and this position, no one can go to the bathroom. The problem is you know that someone has a clipboard and a chart with your name on it and is keeping track of how much fluid you pass or if your bowels have moved. If you don't pass or they don't move, then neither will you. God help you if you have a hemorrhoid or signs of blood in your stool. This will immediately put into action a barrage of tests. One of them is a cold metal object they stick where God never intended anything to be stuck. So you hope for the lesser of the two evils: the IV adventure.

I think it is really a test of your coordination. You try to get out of bed, hold the back of your hospital gown together, and push the IV pole with you to the bathroom. You try not to trip or step on the tube and pull out the needle. The tricky part comes when you try to arrange it just right so that when you sit down, you don't trip, knock over the IV pole, or let your hospital gown hang in the toilet. When I think of this, the fact that we don't have a downstairs bathroom in our house doesn't bother me anymore.

There is another thing we should be thankful for. None of the major TV networks have come up with a show called "America's Most Embarrassing Moment Videos." If there were, Americans all over the country would spend every Sunday night watching other Americans—of all shapes and sizes—getting hospital sponge baths. I have never had the desire to have anyone give me a sponge bath. Maybe candlelight, bubbles, and wine—but not hospital lights, metal pans, and a partner who is fully clothed.

All these thoughts crossed my mind during a five-hour wait at the hospital. Some of the greatest healing that happens in hospitals around the world happens with the visitors. Watching what you could be doing makes doing what you choose to do a lot better. We complain about our lives, our jobs, our relationships, our financial statuses, and the status of the world. The status of those things is the direct result of the choices you've made. Whoever said, "If you have your health, you have everything," was half-right. If you have your health, you still can make choices and change the status of your life, job, relationships, financial status, and the state of your world. But you must make choices to do it. If you don't have your health, that's where the "have tos" start.

If the first thing you think about when you get up in the morning is having to do this or having to do that, stop by the local hospital and see what the real "have tos" are all about. Even in a healthy state, there are things that we have to do. The trick is choosing the end result you are looking for. If you do, you will control the "have tos." They will not control you.

By the way, rumor has it that Fred Bowman's wife doesn't allow him to smoke in the house anymore. Maybe while Mrs. Bowman was visiting Fred in the hospital, she learned something about the "have tos" too.

Gum

Lonnie Donegan sang a song called "Does Your Chewing Gum Lose Its Flavor on the Bedpost Overnight?" I don't know the answer to that question because I have never had the urge to stick a piece of gum on the bedpost and then wake up the next morning to put it back in my mouth. However, sometimes we treat our dreams and goals like the people who start chewing gum and discard it for a new piece as soon as it starts to lose its flavor.

As soon as we run up against obstacles, our goals seem to lose their flavor—and we move on to new ones. We will never reach our dreams without doing the work, and sometimes, the work is hard. There are steps to your dreams. Take them. Life has a way of not showing you how close you are to them sometimes. If you take the next step, you'll find out you're there. If you want to keep throwing away your gum, that's fine, but hold on to your dreams. Your dreams will become your reality.

You'll Never Know Love until You Surrender to It

Someone said, "You'll never know love until you surrender to it." When I thought about that, I realized how everything we do in life that means anything is the same way. If we are not willing to put our all in it, trust it, and relish in its potential, we will never be free to experience its full passion.

That passion will bring you through the trials and tests. We hold back because we are afraid of being hurt or disappointed. The thing we should fear is holding back. By not giving ourselves totally to something, we never fully experience it—and we take strength away from its ability to survive. So surrender to your loves, your dreams, and your hopes. Some of them may not turn out, but by surrendering your whole self, most of them will. The ones that don't, you will have experienced their fullness if only for a small time, which is better than not experiencing them at all.

When I get caught up in man's world of egos and expectations, my soul is prisoner to my body. It looks out the windows of my eyes in loneliness. However, when I share compassion, a smile, a touch, or a word with another, it sets my soul free to touch and be touched by another. When we feel lonely, our souls are telling us that we need to share with another. Sometimes we fear giving of ourselves, but our only fear should be holding back and imprisoning ourselves in loneliness.

I Plugged It In and Took It for Granted

I plugged it in and then took it for granted—until the ice storm of 1998 got my attention.

For days, it rained ice. People were stranded without power, heat, or lights. Some were lucky enough to have kerosene heaters. Others had nothing to fall back on and suffered because of it. The thought struck me how sometimes our relationships with our lovers are like that. Life has a way of getting busy with kids, bills, and other responsibilities, and we drift apart. When the storms of life come and get our attention, we need something to fall back on.

We need the strength for times we hurt and can't say anything. We need someone to gently reach out, hold our hands, and say, "I love you." We find the strength when they—for no reason—reach over, softly touch our faces, and smile. We find the strength when we sit at home together and laugh at a silly movie or cry at a sad one. Those are the times that hold us together and make us realize how lucky we are.

The storms of life will come and go. The secret is to remain standing at the end, holding hands. Love is the gift we give ourselves when we give it away.

You Need to Feed the Robin

One of the first signs of spring in northern New York, where I come from, is when you begin to see the robins. In the springtime, all the birds migrate north after a long, cold winter. Along with this welcome sight comes an opportunity. If you make a wish when you see the first robin in the spring, it will come true.

I make a particular wish each year, but I can't tell you what it is because it will not come true if I tell you. The other day, I was looking out my kitchen window, and a robin landed on the fence. For a moment, I forgot I had already seen one the previous week and made a wish. I was so excited—until I remembered I had done it already.

I turned to go get some birdseed, and a thought struck me: *I have to feed the robin.* I realized there was more to that thought than the bird outside. I realized it meant we have to feed our dreams and wishes with action and belief to have them come true. Until next time, spread a little birdseed each day on the path to your dream.

The Thought Struck Me

I never thought of myself as being brave. As a matter of fact, like most of us, I sometimes feel afraid and insecure. A line in a movie changed my mind, and it may change yours as well. It went something like this: Superman is not brave. He may be strong and good-looking, but he is not brave. The actor said, "Superman is not brave because he is indestructible."

Humans are destructible, but we go out and keep trying. Sometimes it hurts, and sometimes we fail, but we go on in life. We do our best and keep getting back up. We keep living and taking chances for what we believe in.

Someone said once that life wasn't meant to be easy. I thank God that we have these hardships because without knowing hurt, we would never know the full passion of knowing joy, love, or determination. Even though we may not live the storybook form of a brave hero, we know the ecstasy of succeeding because we know the hurt of having to start over. Till next time, my brave friend.

A Diamond in the Rough

When a diamond is born out of the earth, it parallels love stories that last forever. In the beginning, it's exciting. However, the true beauty within the rough diamond can never be brought out unless the diamond cutter took the risk of cutting and polishing it. There is a possibility that it may break in the process. Sometimes there are rough spots to cut through, but once those are dealt with, you see that the true, deeper beauty is greater than you ever imagined.

In essence, the shaping of the diamond symbolizes the nature of love. When we fully give to another, we take a risk. Yet if we fail to, we take a bigger one. When we allow ourselves to be vulnerable, we take a chance. Yet, it's in that vulnerability that we find peace, we find love.

CPSIA information can be obtained at www.ICGtesting.com
Printed in the USA
BVOW08s1541111015

421840BV00001B/2/P